Kev was sitting on the wall.

Sam ran up the hill.

“Hello, Kev!” said Sam.
He got up onto the wall.

“Hop it, kid!” said Kev.
He hit the wall with his cap.

“I like your cap, Kev,” said Sam.

“Hop it, kid, will you?” said Kev.

“Do you like my football?” said Sam.

"Hop it, I tell you!" said Kev.

Kev got so mad with Sam that he fell off the wall.

Kev got up and Sam ran away.

Sam hid by a van.

Kev ran up to the van.

"I said hop it, kid!" said Kev.

Kev's mum was in the van.

Kev's mum was mad.

"Hop it, Kev!" said Sam.